# THE U.S. COAST GUARD

**Nancy Warren Ferrell**

Lerner Publications Company ▪ Minneapolis

*The author is grateful to Dr. Robert L. Scheina,
Historian, U.S. Coast Guard, Washington, D.C., for
his help in assuring the accuracy of this book.
Special thanks to Rear Admiral Edward Nelson, Jr.;
Coast Guard personnel in both Juneau and Sitka, Alaska,
particularly: Rick Benson, Ken Edwards, Mike Hilley,
Ed Moreth, Greg Robinson, and Christopher Haley.
Thanks also to the many Coast Guard personnel who
supplied photographs for this book.*

Library of Congress Cataloging-in-Publication Data

Ferrell, Nancy Warren.
  The U.S. Coast Guard / Nancy Ferrell.
    p.  cm. — (Lerner's armed services series)
  Bibliography: p.
  Includes index.
  Summary: Presents a history of the Coast Guard, outlines its many
duties, and gives information on enlistment benefits.
    ISBN 0-8225-1431-1 (lib. bdg.)
    1. United States. Coast Guard—Juvenile literature. 2. United
States. Coast Guard—Vocational guidance—Juvenile literature.
[1. United States. Coast Guard. 2. United States. Coast Guard—
Vocational guidance. 3. Vocational guidance.] I. Title.
II. Title: United States Coast Guard.  III. Series.
VG53.F47  1989
359.9'7'02373—dc 19
                                          88-19926
                                            CIP
                                              AC

Manufactured in the United States of America

2  3  4  5  6  7  8  9  10  98  97  96  95  94  93  92  91  90  89

# CONTENTS

*Dedicated to:*
*Bill and Patty*
*and*
*to Coast Guard*
*men and women around the world*

# Introduction

The midnight of October 4, 1980, was calm and cold in the Gulf of Alaska. Like a jewel in the blackness, the tourist ship *Prinsendam* glided through the water. Light, carefree music drifted over the waves. The ship, 200 miles (322 kilometers) from the closest port of Yakutat, carried over 500 passengers and crew. This peaceful scene would soon be shattered.

Deep in the core of the ship, in a corner of the engine room, a small fire smoldered and grew. In spite of the crew's efforts, the blaze continued to burn out of control. Several hours later, Captain Cornelius Wabeke sent an SOS to the closest Coast Guard rescue station—Kodiak, over 400 miles away. The distress signal reached not only Kodiak, but Coast Guard stations Sitka and Juneau, Elmendorf Air Force Base in Anchorage, Canadian Rescue in British Columbia, and the oil supertanker *Williamsburg*, which was in the Gulf at the time. Within moments, each of these stations had sent help.

At approximately 5:00 A.M., the *Prinsendam* captain gave the order to abandon ship. The passengers, mostly tourists in their 60s and 70s, were lowered into lifeboats and rafts.

During the next few hours, several rescue vessels arrived at the distress site and located the lifeboats. The rescue forces then began a "daisy-chain" airlift, wherein rescue victims were hoisted from water to helicopter to ship. All through the day and part of the night, survivors were flown to the *Williamsburg* or to the closest coastal towns. In spite of age, cold, heavy seas, fog, hunger, and rain not one life was lost!

Such was the happy ending of one of the largest air-sea rescues in history. The Coast Guard, working alongside other rescue teams, played a major role.

Although search and rescue work is extremely important, it is only one duty of the U.S. Coast Guard. The Service is foremost a branch of the military, working side by side with the Navy in times of war.

Even wartime duties are not the greatest of the Coast Guard's responsibilities. The broad orange markings on

Coast Guard vessels can spell relief for accident victims or trouble for those breaking marine laws. Besides search and rescue, Coast Guard personnel are responsible for marine law enforcement, marine and port safety, environmental protection, and the upkeep of navigational aids. The Coast Guard is the only military service that regularly performs both peacetime as well as wartime duties.

The Coast Guard is a small but dedicated force which began with 10 ships, the biggest no more than 50 feet long, almost 200 years ago.

*Boatyard at the Harbor Entrance, Trouville,* by J.B. Corot (1795-1875), the Fogg Art Museum, Harvard University, Cambridge.

The Coast Guard maintains a commitment to its historical roots as well as to its technological future. Cadets at the Coast Guard Academy learn to sail and to navigate using only the stars. Their terms of service, however, will be spent aboard modern ships that make use of sophisticated equipment.

# 1
# The Cutter Years

In 1790, the first U.S. census was taken. This population survey revealed that the United States had about 4 million residents—roughly the population of Los Angeles, California, today. The majority of these people were living either on or near the East Coast. The new nation's lawmakers realized that as the country expanded, hospitals and schools would have to be built, and roads would have to be constructed. And these needs were only two of the most basic to be met. Yet the new country was quite poor.

In order to raise money, Congress passed the first Tariff Act in 1789. This act provided for a tax on all goods coming into the U.S.—tea, glass, oil, paper, etc. Alexander Hamilton was appointed by George Washington as the first secretary of the treasury for the United States. It was Hamilton's job to handle the country's new revenues.

Not all shippers, however, wanted to pay this tariff. Some smuggled goods to shore to avoid paying the tax. Hamilton asked Congress for 10 ships to patrol the coast and prevent smuggling. Congress approved the request and spent about $1,000 per sailing ship. The men who eventually captained these ships and served aboard them were part of a new agency which became known as the Revenue Marine. And the new agency was effective. During the first 10 years of operation, the exports and imports of the country rose from $52 million to $205 million. The tax on these goods helped Alexander Hamilton pay the bills.

So it was that on August 4, 1790, the U.S. Coast Guard was launched. (The Service, at that time, was known simply as a system of "cutters," or fast ships that "cut" through the water.) Through rich times and poor, and through several name changes over the years, the Service has survived. Today nearly 200 years old, the U.S. Coast Guard is the nation's oldest continuous seagoing force.

Patrolling the entire 2,000 miles of the East Coast was an impossible job for 10 tiny, wind-powered ships. Although the Revenue Marine took on the task eagerly, a more substantial force was clearly needed. Therefore, almost eight years after the Coast Guard came into being, the U.S. Navy was created. Congress decided that whenever it seemed advisable (such as in wartime), the President could place the Revenue Marine under the order of the Navy. This arrangement continues to the present day. In times of peace, the Coast Guard operates under a civilian agency, but in times of war or national emergency the Service is transferred to the Navy.

The early Revenue Marine forces were kept busy. The Service fought in the War of 1812. After that they took on slave traders, then pirates, and then American Indians. Later, in 1846, the Revenue Marine fought in the war with Mexico.

It was during those early beginnings that a pattern was set which shaped the Coast Guard of today. When a marine need arose, and there was no one else to do it, the Coast Guard filled the order. Soon, the Service was performing hundreds of vital—and very different—functions.

Thus, when scientists required transportation or a home base at sea, Revenue Marine cutters took on the job. In fact, the famous naturalist and artist John J. Audubon made two

The cutter *Harriet Lane* was one of the first steamships commissioned by the U.S. government. Steam power was of great importance during combat—it allowed ships to move quickly against the wind.

trips on Revenue Marine cutters when he did his paintings for the book *Birds of America*. In its two centuries of operation, the Coast Guard has assisted many branches of science—biology, medicine, geology, geography, and especially oceanography.

In 1837, when unseasonably stormy weather threatened the East Coast and became a danger to shipping, the Revenue Marine was ordered by Congress to stay at sea and help any vessels in trouble. This single assignment expanded over the years into the countless search and rescue activities so ably handled by the Coast Guard today.

In 1861, the Revenue Marine found itself involved in the Civil War. The *Harriet Lane*, a steamship lent by the Revenue Marine to the Navy, arrived May 9 at Fort Sumter in Charleston harbor and fired the first shot of the war from a naval vessel. (In the early 1800s, wooden sailing ships had begun to give way to metal, steam-powered ships.)

Although railroads and industry centered growth on inland projects after the Civil War, shipping and boat building increased too. Americans became restless and began reaching farther west—and north.

When U.S. Secretary of State William Seward bought the Territory of Alaska from Russia in 1867, the purchase had a major effect on the Revenue Service. Since much of Alaska was uncharted, Congress could not know that by buying Alaska, they had more than doubled the total U.S. coastline. They were soon to learn. Scientists sailing on Revenue ships (by then the agency had been renamed the Revenue Cutter Service) made a rough survey of the land and reported back to Washington, D.C. Congress, in turn, gave the Service more duties: patrolling the new area, protecting the seals and fish, and preventing liquor sales to the Native Americans and Eskimos. Cutters served as courtrooms, hospitals, jails, and churches. Cutters did what needed doing whether the task was officially their responsibility or not.

Icebreakers—ships designed specifically to sail through thick ice—allowed the Coast Guard to map and explore the Alaskan coastline. Since the days of sailing ships, icebreakers have become floating fortresses. The Coast Guard icebreaker *Polar Star*, for instance, has special metal plating on its bow which allows the ship to break through ice 21 feet thick.

13

Near the close of the nineteenth century, the United States fought and won a war on two oceans—the Spanish-American War of 1898. The Atlantic fleet under Commodore William Sampson was placed around Cuba, and the Pacific fleet under Commodore George Dewey fought in the Philippines. The Revenue Cutter Service assisted both fleets.

Then, as the new century was born, so was wireless radio. Because of this discovery, the sea, and eventually the air, would never again hold quite the same mystery or danger. Radio helped to prevent sea disasters as well as to increase the efficiency of rescue work.

The *Titanic*, a British steamer, was the largest ship in the world when it was built. Experts considered the ship unsinkable. On its very first voyage, however, the "unsinkable" *Titanic* went down about 500 miles from the Newfoundland coast.

When the *Titanic* drama took place on April 14, 1912, it only emphasized the need for sea rescue work. On that night, the oceanliner *Titanic* struck an iceberg off the banks of Newfoundland, Canada. Over 1,500 passengers died in the tragedy. It was then that the Revenue Cutter Service took on yet another duty—the International Ice Patrol. This patrol watches for icebergs and warns other ships when icebergs drift into shipping routes. Except during the war years when the patrol was stopped briefly, no vessel has been lost to icebergs in the North Atlantic since this patrol began.

Weeks before the *Titanic* disaster, a sea rescue had occurred that used both the skills of the Lifesaving Service—the "surfmen" who operated lifeguard stations and small shore rescue bases—and the Cutter Service. Surfmen worked from the beach side, while cutters reached survivors from the deep-water side. Joining the two services seemed a logical marriage. So early in 1915, the two services were made one, under the modern name of the United States Coast Guard.

With the history and personnel of the Lifesaving Service came the slogan adopted by the Coast Guard today—"You have to go out." Many years ago, as the story goes, an old keeper of one of the lifesaving stations along the East Coast was about to launch a surf boat to go to the aid of a ship being wrecked on a nearby reef. A storm was pounding, and the water was wild. A person watching said to the keeper, "You're not going out in a sea like that, are you?"

"Yes, I am," replied the keeper.

"Well, you don't expect to come back, do you?"

"I don't know anything about coming back," the keeper answered. "All I know is that the regulations say you have to go out. They don't say anything about coming back."

# 2
# The Modern Coast Guard

On the morning of April 6, 1917, the United States declared war on Germany. A few hours later, a three-word message went out by radio, telephone, and mail to all Coast Guard units:

"Plan One Acknowledge."

This brief dispatch officially placed the Coast Guard under the arm of the Navy. America had entered World War I. Coast Guard cutters, small and speedy, were extremely useful in convoying transports and hunting submarines during the following 19 months until the war's end.

One of the most serious disasters of the war and of Coast Guard history occurred on September 26, 1918. The cutter *Tampa*, a hard-working vessel based in Gibraltar, had just completed a convoy mission and was heading for a base in Great Britain. Suddenly, men on nearby vessels heard a great explosion. Since the *Tampa* never arrived at its destination, experts believe that a German U-boat sank the ship. Only a little wreckage was ever recovered. All hands on the *Tampa* were killed, including 111 Coast Guard members. The loss of the *Tampa* was the largest loss of life by any U.S. Navy unit during the war.

Not all Coast Guard work dealt with convoying transports in the war zone. Lifesaving stations along the U.S. eastern seaboard provided eyes and ears to warn against submarines approaching American shores. Always alert to sabotage, Coast Guard members supervised the loading of explosives

**Sunk by a German submarine in 1918, the *USCG Tampa* remains a powerful symbol of Coast Guard sacrifice.**

and ammunition in important Atlantic ports. This duty eventually grew into the Port Security agency, yet another job of the Coast Guard today. Because of the Coast Guard's care during World War I, no port under its supervision had even a minor explosion or lost a single life.

After the war, the Coast Guard was once again signed into the Treasury Department for peacetime duties.

Almost overnight, the Coast Guard found itself in another war of sorts—this time at home. The passage of the Prohibition Act in 1919 made it illegal to use, sell, or import alcoholic beverages in the U.S. The Coast Guard, armed with additional boats and men, was charged with stopping seagoing "rumrunners," as smugglers were called. Alcohol smuggling was heaviest along the East Coast, where most of the population lived.

Just because the Coast Guard was extra busy during Prohibition did not mean it neglected its other duties. Quite the opposite held true. New duties were added by Congress, such as enforcing the Alaskan game laws and the new regulations about polluting waters with oil.

In 1927, a series of floods in the Ohio, Illinois, and Mississippi River valleys endangered thousands of people. Far from their normal saltwater territory, the Coast Guard patrolled the flooded areas. They looked for trouble spots, brought in workers, materials, supplies, and food, and transported thousands of people to safety.

In 1939, the U.S. Lighthouse Service proved another logical addition to the Coast Guard's resources. With the new agency came experienced people, thousands of aids to navigation, lightships, lighthouses, tenders, and icebreakers.

When the United States entered World War II in 1941, the Coast Guard was ordered to work with the Navy once again. Besides search and rescue work, the Guard performed anti-submarine warfare escort, beach patrol, port security, weather duty, and landings on enemy territory. Not only did experienced Coast Guard surfmen handle boats for amphibious landings, but they trained other military services too. Coast Guard forces helped to coordinate beach landings in Italy, Africa, and France, as well as in the Aleutians and other islands of the Pacific. More than 240,000 Coast Guard personnel served the Allied cause in World War II. These numbers were swelled by a strong force of auxiliaries— volunteers who agree to help the Service in emergencies.

Women joined up as well. In 1942, the Women's Reserve— SPARs—was established. (The name SPAR is made up of both Latin and English initials of the Coast Guard motto:

*Semper Paratus*—Always Ready.) These women, numbering over 10,000, worked dozens of jobs which released men for sea duty.

The Coast Guard officially returned to the Treasury Department after the war, on January 1, 1946.

Only four years after World War II, the Korean hostilities attracted world headlines. Because this conflict was considered a "police action," and not an official war, the Coast Guard was not transferred to the Navy in 1950. Nevertheless, the Coast Guard operated reserve stations throughout the Pacific Ocean to protect the troops sent into combat. Coast Guard experts also trained the Korean Navy.

The situation was much the same during the Vietnam War. Coast Guard members inspected Vietnamese boats for smuggled goods or people, provided gunfire support for U.S. forces, escorted convoy ships into the country, built search stations for U.S. warplane rescue, and set up a system of navigational aids to prevent ship accidents.

The *USCG Point Hudson*, shown here in 1966 on its way to South Vietnam, was only one of many 82-foot patrol boats to participate in the Vietnam War.

In spite of international conflicts, the Coast Guard continued doing its other jobs. One duty—icebreaking—led to another first in history.

In 1957, Coast Guard cutters *Spar*, *Bramble*, and *Storis* were working their way toward the Atlantic Ocean through heavy ice, north of Point Barrow, Alaska. Finally, on September 3, the *Spar* met a Canadian icebreaker working west to meet them. The three Coast Guard ships had found the deep-water Northwest Passage for which explorers had been searching for centuries. When the *Spar* finally reached its home base in Rhode Island, it became the first American ship to sail completely around the North American continent.

In 1967, official control of the Coast Guard was transferred from the Treasury Department to the Department of Transportation, where it remains today. Although some duties, such as most lighthouse jobs, have been automated, the Coast Guard continues to perform other duties. Between 1970 and 1980, Congress passed more than 30 laws giving new or expanded responsibilities, sole or shared, to the Coast Guard.

And then, in 1976, a 200-mile fishing conservation zone was established off the coast of the United States. The United States reserves the right to control how many fish are caught in this area. This expanded zone quadrupled the area which the Coast Guard patrols and in which it enforces marine law.

# 3
# The Coast Guard Takes to the Air

When the famous Wright brothers took the first 59-second airplane flight at Kitty Hawk in 1903, Coast Guardsmen were on hand. In fact, they actually *gave* a hand. Three Lifesavers from the Kill Devil Lifeboat Station in North Carolina helped carry the biplane to the launch site.

**This HH-52A helicopter, sitting atop a Coast Guard cutter, is preparing for flight.**

The Wright Brothers, Orville (*left*) and Wilbur (*right*), constructed and flew the first motor-driven airplane. Their first flight lasted just under one minute.

A dozen years passed before the Coast Guard took a more hands-on approach to flying. Lieutenants Elmer Stone and Norman Hall—both assigned to the cutter *Onondaga*—often talked about how much more of the ocean could be viewed from a plane on rescue missions. With the backing of their commanding officer, Lt. Stone and five other men were assigned to the Naval Aviation School in Florida in 1916.

The same Lt. Stone flew one of the most famous airplane flights in history. In 1919, Stone of the Coast Guard, Captain A.C. Reade of the Navy, and a Navy crew made the first successful transatlantic crossing. Stone's flight came eight years before Charles Lindbergh's solo flight.

With Prohibition in the 1920s, air power was needed to help combat whiskey smuggling. Planes could spot boats hidden in coves along the coastline, and they could go much faster than any ship. Congress finally appropriated money for five aircraft in 1926. Although law enforcement duties nudged the Coast Guard into the air, the Service used its new planes for other important activities as well—mapping underwater channels, operating search and rescue missions, providing weather information, and flying iceberg patrol, to mention only a few.

By the time World War II began, the Coast Guard had a small but effective flying unit. Usually, Coast Guard planes flew patrols for weather information and rescue work. But as enemy submarines began lurking near U.S. shores, the planes were armed with depth charges (explosives designed to sink rapidly and destroy underwater targets). One Coast Guard amphibious craft actually sank a German submarine in the Gulf of Mexico.

**Not only did Lieutenant Elmer Stone pioneer the use of aircraft in rescue work, he also made the first trans-Atlantic flight in May 1919.**

Also during World War II, the helicopter came into its own. Though this new invention was at first slated for search and rescue work, military officers soon saw its application to antisubmarine warfare. Coast Guard personnel not only trained U.S. helicopter pilots at the Brooklyn Air Station, but they ended up training all Allied helicopter pilots as well.

Today's Coast Guard relies as heavily on air power as on sea power. State-of-the-art communications equipment allows for perfect coordination between ships, planes, and helicopters.

The Service first used helicopters during World War II. As helicopters grew larger and more stable, the Coast Guard began to rely on them more for actual rescues, in addition to scouting and patrol.

World War II also generated two electronic developments which affected world travel by sea and by air long after the war was over. Radar, a device which locates an object by projecting radio waves, is well known and has many important functions.

The other electronic development—LORAN—was more complicated. LORAN, which stands for LOng Range Aid to Navigation, was devised by a team of researchers and named by Coast Guard Captain Lawrence Harding during the war. In a nutshell, LORAN uses radio stations to send out electronic impulses. Whether on a plane or ship, a navigator sending an electronic signal and measuring the signal's return time with a LORAN chart is able to pinpoint the vessel's location with remarkable accuracy. By 1944, thanks in part to cooperation with the British and Canadian navies, the North Atlantic sported many LORAN stations. It wasn't long before the Pacific had its share as well.

After World War II, helicopters, LORAN, and radar were put to peacetime use. LORAN stations multiplied rapidly. (By the late 1980s, the number of LORAN stations had increased to 34.) Helicopters soon became standard equipment for rescue bases. Some rescue missions required helicopters. This fact was brought home during a series of floods in New England in 1955. In order to rescue stranded victims, helicopters were forced to hover between telephone poles, trees, and antennas of all kinds.

Coast Guard pilots were active during the Korean and Vietnam wars, primarily on rescue missions; pilots were among the 8,000 Coast Guard personnel who served in Vietnam. It was a helicopter which plucked *Prinsendam* survivors from the heavy seas of Alaska in 1980.

Today, a Coast Guard pilot from the *Prinsendam* rescue mission has been selected for another Service first. Lieutenant Commander Bruce Melnick was chosen to be the first Coast Guardsman to train for the National Aeronautics and Space Administration (NASA) astronaut program in Houston, Texas.

This HRP-1 helicopter, built and commissioned in 1948, cost $256,000.00 — small change in comparison with the pricetags of today's helicopters.

# 4
# Joining the Coast Guard

If you live in Hawaii, by a sea coast, near the Great Lakes, or along the Mississippi River, you have probably heard of the Coast Guard before now. If you live inland, away from any large waterway, you may not have. The Coast Guard is a small, efficient military and peacetime force with the strength of about 40,000 men and women on active duty. Add to this about 12,000 reserves, 6,000 civilian workers, and 40,000 auxiliary volunteers, and you have the complete picture.

The "how" to join the Coast Guard is easy—see a recruiter. The "why" is more personal.

Very few young men and women leaving high school know exactly what work they want to do with their lives. Some want to get away from home and become independent. Some want training or schooling before selecting a career. Some want to try different jobs before making a lifetime choice. The military—any of the armed services—answers these needs. All services offer training, career choices, schooling, and a chance to live independently. For some young people, the military is the way to go. And for some of those, the service itself may be the final career choice until retirement.

Then why the Coast Guard?

Because the Coast Guard is different.

The Coast Guard is well trained and does its share during wartime, but its primary focus is on peacetime activities—helping people. Coast Guard men and women are proud of

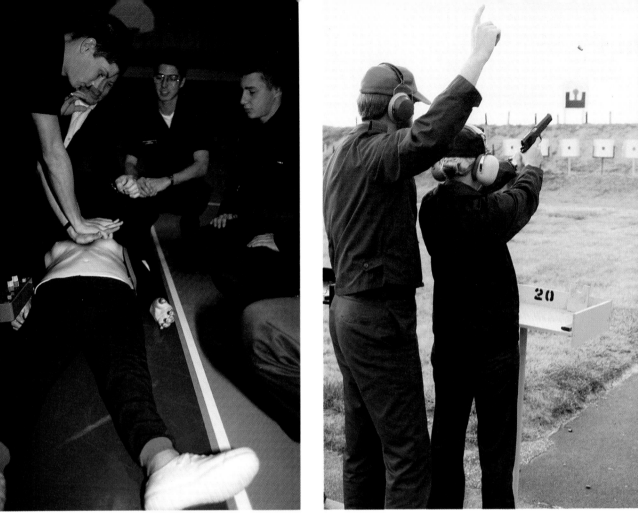

Lifesaving courses (*left*) occupy fully as much of a recruit's time as target practice (*right*). The Coast Guard functions as both the "ambulance" and the "police force" of the sea. Personnel must be fully prepared for both types of duty.

the humanitarian side of the Service. While search and rescue headlines such as "Coast Guard Saves Crash Victims in Three-Hour Drama" capture most of the attention, there are a full range of other peacetime services that the Coast Guard provides. And each Coast Guard person, as a member of a well-trained team, helps other team members.

## The Benefits

If you join the Coast Guard, you are eligible for certain benefits: a paycheck twice a month, with extra money for uniforms and for your dependents if you have a family; housing and meals, or a food and housing allowance; free medical and dental care; a low-cost insurance policy; an opportunity to travel; 30 days of vacation a year; and a chance to participate in Veterans Administration programs, some of which help with further training or college expenses. If you decided to make the Coast Guard your career, you would be eligible for retirement after 20 years of service.

## The Requirements

Anyone wishing to join the Coast Guard must fulfill certain requirements:

1. Must be between the ages of 17 and 26 years
2. Must be a U.S. citizen, or must have filed a Declaration of Intent to become a citizen
3. Must meet certain mental, physical, and character standards.

A high school senior can enlist and wait up to 12 months before going on active duty. Anyone out of school can sign on and wait up to half a year. The months between signing the enlistment and going on active duty count toward service time. Once signed on, the enlistee is obligated for eight years (two or four active, plus six or four inactive, as a ready reserve).

A person joining the Coast Guard or any other U.S. military service must take the basic ASVAB test (Armed Services Vocational Aptitude Battery). The ASVAB helps an individual measure his or her own readiness to acquire a skill or ability. Three of the test sections deal with aptitude or potential for higher learning; four measure aptitude in occupational areas. Using the test results, personal interests, school grades, and achievements, a military advisor can help the enlistee choose a career suited to his or her talents.

To give you an idea of the questions on the ASVAB, two are listed below:

1. The wind is *variable* today. (Word Knowledge)

    1-A. mild

    1-B. steady

    1-C. shifting

    1-D. chilling

2. How many 36-passenger buses will it take to carry 144 people? (Mathematical Reasoning)

    2-A. 3

    2-B. 4

    2-C. 5

    2-D. 6

These opportunities, tests, requirements, and benefits apply to women too. The Coast Guard, unlike the other four military services, allows women to serve in direct combat in times of war. The Guard feels that women are as much a part of the team as men, and that means *all* of the time. Both men and women do their jobs and carry their own share of the work load.

Suppose you take the test and want to go further. You have fulfilled the requirements. You decide to sign on the dotted line for your first tour of duty, or period of enlistment. The Coast Guard pays your way, and you are off to eight weeks training at boot camp—Cape May, New Jersey.

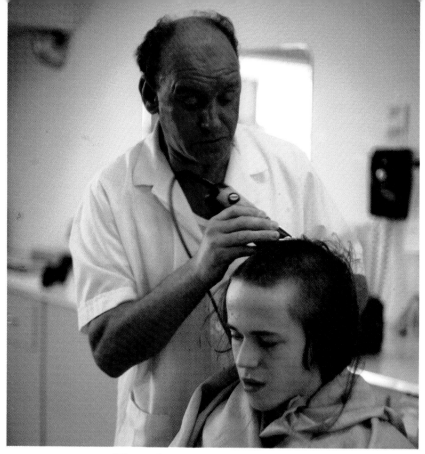
The military haircut comes first.

## Boot Camp

Boot camp is tough. The training begins with concentrated discipline to catch the recruit's attention. After three days at boot camp, many recruits wish they could turn around and take the bus back home. But the recruits stick with it. And when they are done with the eight weeks, they often say it was the most fulfilling time of their lives.

The first few days at camp deal with haircuts, dental and physical exams, fitting uniforms, and filling out forms. Then begins an intensive physical training program. Since Coast Guard work is centered on or near the water, recruits are taught to swim. The following weeks are concerned with seamanship, advanced first aid, controlling fires, handling weapons, target practice, and much more. But it is not all work—there are relaxing times along the way. At the end of boot camp, a recruit has earned the rank of E-2.

A recruit who has already served in another military force can forego the basic military training of boot camp and concentrate on the classes only. Previous military experience may count toward Coast Guard advancement.

The underlying goal of boot camp is learning to work together. Here, as in all fields of Coast Guard work, teamwork is the key word. And when graduation finally comes, it is a day of celebration with family and a time of immense pride.

**By the eighth week, a class of new recruits works together as a team.**

Near the end of the program, a counselor helps each recruit focus on a job that interests him or her and for which the recruit is qualified. There are a variety of jobs to choose from. Listed below are samples of job classifications, or ratings, with related civilian jobs:

| Coast Guard Rating | Related Civilian Job |
| --- | --- |
| Radar Operator | air traffic controller, radio operator, missile tracking specialist |
| Gunner's Mate | gunsmith, locksmith, machinist, hydraulic equipment mechanic |
| Damage Controller | firefighter, carpenter, construction supervisor, safety engineer, building superintendent |
| Machinery Technician | auto mechanic, refrigeration specialist, machinist |
| Public Affairs Specialist | professional photographer, news reporter, freelance writer, layout artist |
| Storekeeper | bookkeeper, purchasing agent, shipping clerk, warehouse clerk |
| Radio Operator | computer operator, radio dispatcher, telegrapher, telecommunications manager |
| Subsistence Specialist | restaurant manager, baker, caterer |
| Health Services Technician | X-ray technician, medical/ dental technician, pharmaceutical salesperson |

| Yeoman | legal clerk, court reporter, word processor, executive secretary, personnel manager |
| Marine Science Technician | weather forecaster, meteorologist's assistant, marine environmental specialist |
| Electronics Technician | electronics technician, computer technician, telephone/radio/radar technician |

Coast Guard men and women receive the same pay and are divided into the same ranks as their counterparts in the Navy. (For a complete listing of Coast Guard ranks, see the Appendix on page 70.)

## What It's Like

Suppose you are fresh out of boot camp, with your basic training behind you. You talk to a Coast Guard career counselor and decide that you might like eventually to qualify as a machinery technician. Instead of going to a specialized training school right away, you opt first for a duty station (any active Coast Guard station) where you can learn on the job. You suggest the location you prefer, and the Coast Guard checks to see if there is an opening there.

You might, for instance, be sent to Juneau, Alaska.

Station Juneau is situated in a small building alongside Gastineau Channel in the downtown section of the capital. The unit is a search and rescue lifeboat station, operated by 14 people. Their equipment consists of a 4-wheel-drive, radio-equipped pickup; a van; a 41-foot utility boat; a 25-foot Boston Whaler; and an 11-foot inflatable Zodiak raft.

Coast Guard Station Juneau is located on the waterfront in Juneau, Alaska. The city of Juneau is surrounded by steep mountains and the huge Tongass National Forest. Coast Guard members stationed in this beautiful northern location enjoy year round a landscape that is the envy of tourists.

Polished, tuned, and fueled, the 41-foot Coast Guard rescue boat rides at the dock outside Station Juneau. A "Mayday" signal coming over the station's radio will bring a rescue team pouring onto the boat, and within seconds the dock will be empty.

The Coast Guard would help you find a place to stay in Juneau, whether you were single or had a family. All kinds of support groups would help you settle in.

Personnel at the station itself are led by a chief petty officer, a rank similar to sergeant in the Army. The staff is divided into two duty sections, nicknamed "port" and

37

"starboard." There are five people in each duty section:

1 OOD (Officer of the Day and boat leader)

4 boat crew and/or watch standers.

Since you would be new, you would be part of the boat crew.

All personnel put in an 8:00 A.M.-4:00 P.M. day during the week. In addition, the crew "on duty" lives at the station for a forty-eight hour shift. At the end of that time, they live at home for forty-eight hours. (All personnel, however, are on call 24 hours every day in case of emergency.) The members of the duty crew take turns standing watch and working, so each person has time for sleeping and relaxing too. Station Juneau, like most Coast Guard stations, has bunks, a TV, and a small recreation area.

A good part of search and rescue work is waiting. There is no telling when an emergency might occur. During the wait, the duty crew keeps busy with station tasks. One of the duty crew always stays right in the station—for security, answering phone calls, taking messages, and being ready for any incoming emergencies. If the boat crew is out on a call, the person at the station passes information to and from the boat.

One of the other four duty crew members constantly stands watch around the station. The rest complete the endless tasks necessary for keeping up the station—checking equipment on the boat, working on an engine, doing general maintenance work, and so on. In order for search and rescue equipment to be effective, it must be in top shape—from the 41-footer right down to the emergency medical technician's kit.

Besides station duties, all personnel must be scheduled for continued training in weapons, first aid, navigation, survival, law enforcement, and search and rescue techniques—plus practice in each category. Rescue duties could range from fighting a fire on a boat, to finding lost hunters, to giving aid to a cruise passenger with a heart attack. Each member of the Coast Guard must have the required skills and must be ready to use them.

A survivor of a small plane crash north of Cold Bay, Alaska, steps from a Coast Guard rescue helicopter.

Learning to fight fires is extremely important for Coast Guard members. Fire is one of the most common reasons for a ship to sink, and oil tankers and platforms are especially vulnerable.

When the "Mayday" call comes over the radio, everything else stops. The 4-person team takes off for the 41-footer. They are fast, knowing lives depend on their speed. In a recent unscheduled drill, the crew made it from the station, around the station's security fencing, across a block-long dock, down a ramp, onto the boat, got underway, and were ready to fight a boat fire in three minutes! They don't stop to pick up orders, or pull on survival suits, or find out where they are going. They prepare on the way to the site of the emergency. The Coast Guard just moves—and fast!

## Always More Training

Rather than choose a duty station right away, a recruit might decide on further training. A recruit's chosen career in the Service dictates where he or she will go. An enlisted person wanting to focus on fire control, for example, would be sent for 34 weeks of intensive training at the Naval Training Center, Great Lakes, Illinois. Training as an electronics technician would require 23 weeks at Governor's Island, New York. An aviation machinist mate requires 16 weeks of training at the CG Aviation Technical Training Center, Elizabeth City, North Carolina. A storekeeper rating includes a 10-week course at Petaluma, California. Other centers around the United States are open for various Coast Guard job training programs.

If a recruit—man or woman—feels ambitious about schooling, there are several options. He or she can work at a duty station under a petty officer, do some studying outside of work, score well on an exam, and receive both a promotion and a raise in salary.

A recruit who has graduated from college may qualify for Officer Candidate School. If so, he or she would spend 17 weeks at the CG Reserve Training Center in Yorktown, Virginia, earning a commission as an officer.

Correspondence classes while on the job are another educational option. Sometimes an enlisted person can obtain help paying the tuition if he or she attends night classes at a nearby university.

Finally, there is the college program. If a recruit signs up for this program, part of his or her monthly salary is put away for future college study. When and if the Coast Guard member finishes a term of service and goes to college, that recruit's savings will be matched by a contribution from the Coast Guard. Or, before becoming an enlisted recruit, a person can try for the Coast Guard Academy in New London, Connecticut. A major advantage to this option is that recruits graduate from the academy not only with a college degree but also with the rank of an officer.

But a new recruit does not have to attend a formal school to become an officer. The Coast Guard is too small to overlook talent. About one-fifth of those promoted to officer rank come from chief petty officers. These talented people have climbed from enlisted status. There are years of hard work and practical experience behind their titles. With energy and intellect, any individual can reach high rank.


(Answers to the ASVAB questions: 1-C; 2-B)

An aerial view of the
Sitka Coast Guard Air
Station, Alaska

A Coast Guard meteo-
rologist (weatherperson)
studies weather charts
at Kodiak Air Station,
Alaska.

A typical barracks
located at Station Sitka

**USCGC EAGLE**

# 5
# The Coast Guard Academy

Where American Indians and international pirates once landed their boats along the Thames River, now stands the U.S. Coast Guard Academy. The school is situated halfway between Boston and New York at New London, Connecticut. Its buildings are grouped over 120 acres. They are connected by a network of streets named for famous ships of the Service, such as the *Tampa*, the *Bear*, the *Harriet Lane*, and the *Spencer*. Berthed at a dock on the waterfront is the famous CG training square-rigger, the *Eagle*.

The Coast Guard Academy is a four-year accredited (officially recognized) university. About 750 men and women attend the Academy, with approximately 170 graduating each year. Coursework emphasizes engineering, science, and mathematics, but majors in government and management are available. Students graduate with a Bachelor of Science degree.

Unlike the other U.S. military academies, which accept students on the basis of where they come from or because a member of Congress has appointed them, entrance to the Coast Guard Academy is based on annual nationwide competition. Entrance to the Academy depends on SAT or ACT test results, high school class standing, and potential for leadership. Students must be between the ages of 17 and 22, have completed or be about to complete high school,

Cadets march at the Coast Guard Academy, New London, Connecticut.

be U.S. citizens, unmarried, and in good physical and mental condition.

There is no tuition fee, but a $500 deposit is required for initial equipment and clothing costs. One hundred dollars of this money is paid at the time of the appointment and the rest when the candidate reports to the Academy. This fee may be waived in cases where a student's family would find it difficult to pay. The Academy arranges transportation from home to New London.

One real advantage to Academy life is that the federal government pays each student over $5,700 a year for expenses (uniforms, textbooks, equipment) and provides room and board. All students live on campus.

Discipline is stiff, and it has to be. The four years of training must prepare the cadet for immediate responsibilities as a junior officer aboard ship after graduation. The cadet must learn self-control, discipline, and respect for authority.

A typical day at the Academy starts at 6:15 A.M. with breakfast, followed by morning classes, lunch, and afternoon classes, which end at 3:30. The hours until dinner at 6:45 depend on the individual cadet. The time can be filled with sports, extracurricular activities, or extra tutoring. Study time begins at 7:00 and may continue until 10:00. Taps at 10:15 P.M. marks the end of the day. Generally speaking, weekend afternoons and evenings are reserved for liberty, or free time.

The Academy places a strong emphasis on sports. Not only do sports promote good health and fitness, but they teach teamwork—an element required in so many real-life Coast Guard situations. Track, soccer, golf, crew, wrestling, football, sailing, baseball, swimming, tennis, volleyball, and

47

basketball are popular. A number of non-sport activities are also available—art, music, theater, movies, photography, writing, radio, debating, dances, and more.

**Cadets carry teamwork into all aspects of their lives at the Academy. Football is very popular.**

Summer school is a required part of the Academy schedule, but it is not like some people's idea of summer school. After a few weeks of vacation, the summer is devoted to professional training. It is a hands-on program, in which a cadet puts to practical use the lessons she or he has learned during the previous year. There are courses in all phases of military activity, plus fire-fighting, seamanship, and navigation. Some of the training is completed at shore stations away from the

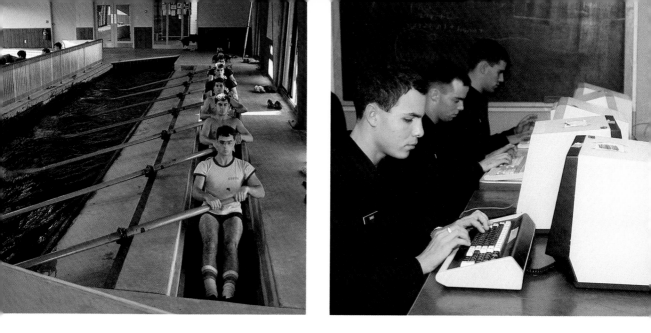

Three phases of
Academy training:
cadets must learn
rowing techniques
(*top, left*); computer
technology is a high
priority, as it has
begun to dominate
shipboard naviga-
tion (*top, right*);
cadets learn tra-
ditional methods
of sailing and
navigating aboard
the *USCG Eagle*
(*bottom*).

Academy. During their last summer, cadets spend five weeks
at various seagoing Coast Guard units, taking part in actual
Coast Guard operations.

**Like any other college or university, the Coast Guard Academy demands devoted study.**

But what everyone seems to look forward to most are the cruises—some short trips, some long. The Academy owns the Yankee bark *Eagle*, which was built in Germany for Hitler's navy in 1936. It later sailed to the U.S. as a prize of war and found a permanent berth at the Academy. Fitted with modern navigational equipment and a diesel engine (named "Elmer"), the square-rigger is a floating classroom teaching practical seamanship. With a crew of over 200 cadets, the *Eagle* cruises to many U.S. and foreign ports. Sailing with the *Eagle* is a definite plus to Academy life.

Upon graduation, a cadet has not only completed a college degree but has earned the title of ensign—a commissioned rank (or officer's rank) in the Coast Guard. The cadet is then expected to serve five years in the Service and can look forward to an interesting and demanding career. Ranks, pay, and allowances on the job are the same as those for officers of equal rank in the other military services.

After a few years of active service as an officer, a person's post-graduate opportunities open up. An officer, for instance, may wish to become a pilot. If so, he or she may qualify for additional training under the direction of Coast Guard and Navy instructors. Or the Service might enroll an officer for further schooling in another leading university somewhere in the country—it would all depend on the officer's interests and skills.

Academy life requires discipline and work, but no cadet is perfect. Take, for example, Worth G. Ross, who was a cadet in the first Academy class. Not only did Ross rack up his share of bad reports at first, but he had some trouble with seasickness. Yet, years later, he became commandant of the Coast Guard.

# 6
# The Law and Safety

It started off as a search and rescue mission but ended as the largest drug bust in Coast Guard history.

The date was May 8, 1987. The setting was the sea around St. Croix, a U.S. island in the Caribbean. An auxiliarist (a Coast Guard volunteer) had run his boat to the area to help search for a missing diver. Also nearby, but overhead, was a helicopter from Boringuen Air Station in Puerto Rico.

While searching the waters, the volunteer came upon a boat—*La Toto*—anchored off the coast in a shallow cove behind a reef. Thinking the boat might be in trouble, the volunteer approached and talked to the captain. The captain's jittery manner and suspicious answers alerted the volunteer.

After shoving off from *La Toto*, the volunteer contacted the helicopter above by radio and reported what he had seen. The pilot checked with his air station and was told that *La Toto* had been previously targeted as a possible smuggler. A C-130 aircraft was sent to the area to keep watch, while the Coast Guard's 110-foot patrol ship *Ocracoke* sped to the location. Once on the scene, the *Ocracoke* launched a small boat, and four men eventually boarded *La Toto*. Two of the Coast Guard party noticed that the fuel tank had been altered. The first of the cocaine was found there. *Ocracoke* seized the vessel and arrested the crew. The boat was escorted to San Juan.

Once they had *La Toto* in port, the Coast Guard team spent 11 hours taking the boat apart. They found package after package of cocaine. As the batches were unloaded, *La Toto* rose higher in the water. On final count, 3,771 pounds of cocaine were removed—street value, $250 million. The street value for that one arrest alone was one-twelfth of the total Coast Guard budget for a year.

Law enforcement is one of the primary duties of the Coast Guard. In 1936, Congress authorized the Coast Guard to enforce all the federal laws on the high seas and on the navigable waters of the U.S. That gave the Coast Guard the power to board foreign vessels in U.S. waters (with the foreign country's permission) and U.S. ships anywhere in the world without a warrant. In truth, the American Coast Guard is the world's largest maritime police force.

**Sensitive instruments in the cockpit of a C-130 aircraft spell trouble for smugglers.**

A Coast Guard crew member unloads bags of narcotics seized in a drug bust in Boston Harbor.

To do its job, the Coast Guard maintains a fleet of vessels. Some are the small 31-foot patrol boats—fast and maneuverable. The different sizes range up to the heavyweights—the 210-, 270-, and the 378-foot cutters. Mix in a variety of sophisticated helicopters and airplanes, and you have a very strong marine patrol force.

However, since drug smugglers are presently shifting operations to the air, and even monitoring Coast Guard patrols, the Service is strengthening its air defense activities. Some patrols now use a Hawkeye aircraft equipped with an electronic radar sensor which spots targets both on the water and in the air.

The smuggling of people has been on the increase too. More and more Coast Guard boats are intercepting illegal aliens—citizens of other countries who enter the United States without permission. Some refugees, for instance, are fleeing from the political unrest in the island country of Haiti. They crowd themselves onto the smallest of boats and

54

try to sail the 600 miles across the Caribbean Sea to the mainland of Florida.

The Coast Guard endurance cutter *Alert* intercepted two tiny sailboats one night, packed from bow to stern with Haitian refugees. One was a 20-foot sailboat with 50 people on board, and the other was a 30-footer with 98 passengers! That would be like cramming 100 people into two 16-foot Ford family vans. A year before, the Coast Guard had stopped a 45-foot sailboat with 228 Haitians aboard!

A continent away from Florida, off the coast of Alaska, another sort of problem exists.

In order to control the world's fishing grounds, the nations of the world have signed a series of treaties. There are thousands of rules concerning how many of what fish species can be caught, where, by what means, and so on. Within the 200-mile limit of sea around the U.S., the Coast Guard is responsible for enforcing such treaties. Foreign vessels must obtain permission to fish within these limits.

The northern Bering Sea and the Gulf of Alaska have long been rich fishing grounds. Because of this abundance, ships from other countries (Poland, Japan, Korea, Russia, China) travel great distances to fish there. The foreign fishing companies process their catches on factory ships and send the product back to their country. This work goes on all year.

Because of the money involved, and the isolation of the huge fishing areas, it is tempting for fishing ships—both foreign and domestic—to catch more fish than they are allowed. It is the Coast Guard's duty to see that they do not. In order to check this, vessels must be boarded and their catches counted. But the prime fishing areas cover millions of square miles, so even locating a ship is not easy.

If the ship has violated the legal limits, the Coast Guard can fine the ship, or actually seize it and its cargo. If a foreign vessel is actually "arrested," international diplomacy is involved. Most often, a vessel's illegal catch is sold to pay the heavy fines that U.S. courts impose on violators of conservation laws.

In 1984, the Coast Guard seized a total of 80 vessels—74 of them foreign—for fishing violations. Many more ships were fined. By being on the scene, the Coast Guard tends to keep the fishing operations more honest.

## Military Preparedness

Peacetime activities are such an important part of Coast Guard work that it is sometimes easy to forget that the Guard is a military service.

The Coast Guard, like other military forces, employs an extra force of men and women which it can call on in case of war or emergency. This extra force is the Reserves, personnel who are trained and able to become full-time Coast Guard members if necessary. Coast Guard reservists, who number over 12,000, drill once a month and during a two-week active-duty period each year. In addition to being on call for emergencies or military alert in their hometowns year-round, they assist in search and rescue work, port security, and other missions.

## Port, Marine, and Boating Safety

It was war that brought waterfront duties to the Coast Guard. Worried about sabotage at U.S. coastal ports during

World War I, Congress gave the Coast Guard the job of making ports secure. Today, inspectors examine commercial vessels for equipment and cargo safety and monitor the daily traffic of vessels in the harbors. Such inspections extend to off-shore oil drilling rigs and production platforms as well.

Because of the traffic in U.S. harbors, port security is no minor job. New York Harbor alone sees the arrival and departure of 7,000 ships a year. Each year the Coast Guard boards over 54,000 vessels and inspects an average of 85,000 shoreside facilities.

Sea captains and their merchant vessels must be licensed, just like drivers and their cars. Mark Twain discovered that over a century ago when he obtained his first steamboat pilot's license. The Coast Guard makes sure that commercial vessels carry adequate lifeboats, fire-fighting equipment, and first aid supplies. Safety is the focus for civilian boating, too. Boats propelled by machinery have to be numbered and must carry safety equipment. In addition, the Service is charged with setting up an educational program for civilians.

The Coast Guard educates and tests civilians with the help of the nearly 40,000 Coast Guard Auxiliary members. The Auxiliary is a volunteer organization made up of civilian men and women, some of them retired Coast Guard people. The organization came into being just before World War II. Auxiliarists inspect boats for safety (at the owner's request) and issue decals which declare the boat safe. In addition, auxiliarists teach courses that include boat operation and the "rules of the road." And, occasionally, they offer their help in rescue work when a large area has to be searched in record time.

Specially-trained personnel, called to the scene of an oil spill, prepare to release a containment boom. The boom expands and floats on the water, trapping oil before it can travel too far.

# 7
# Rescues and More

A 38-foot fishing boat, the *Parks 15*, was returning from a crabbing trip in Shelikof Strait, Alaska, in the fall of 1983. A September storm roared in, stirring up 16-foot seas and gale force winds. The *Parks 15* took on water and began sinking.

The crew of four—Captain Archie Densmore, his daughter Wendi, 19, his granddaughter, 3-year-old Misty Dawn, and Wendi's cousin Melanie, 14—sent out an SOS before the boat capsized and went under.

One radio operator heard the distress signal and notified the Coast Guard air station at Kodiak. A Sikorsky helicopter immediately took off for the search. In addition to the crew, the helicopter carried a hypothermia expert, Coast Guard Doctor Martin Nemiroff, then stationed in Kodiak. Nemiroff was trained to deal with patients whose body temperatures had dropped close to freezing.

After more than an hour, the helicopter spotted red floats in the water and located the survivors. The helicopter had to bob up to miss the 10-foot wave crests, then drop down into the trough. It still managed to pluck Wendi and her cousin from the water. The maneuver was extremely dangerous to the helicopter crew and the craft. Nearby in the water was the lifeless body of 3-year-old Misty Dawn. In spite of the relatives' attempts earlier, first Misty's breathing and then her heart had stopped. For the past 40 minutes before rescue, she had been floating face down in the water. The helicopter crew now lifted her body into the plane.

After rescuing the grandfather, the helicopter swung up and away, heading for Kodiak air base. Once in the air, the doctor began treating the victims.

With little hope, Nemiroff began CPR on Misty, using an oxygen tube in the corner of his mouth. He sucked saltwater from the girl's lungs and breathed warm air back in. Soon he turned the job over to Medical Corpsman Dee Ricard. Then Doctor Nemiroff tried to help the grandfather, whose heart had stopped.

Finally the helicopter reached Kodiak. There an airplane waited on a cleared runway, prepared to take the survivors to an Anchorage hospital. Once down, Nemiroff yelled out the cargo door to bring the ambulance so that the victims could be transferred to the airplane.

"Hurry up," he shouted. "We've got two hypothermic victims, and two on CPR."

Corpsman Ricard looked up. "We just have one on CPR, Doctor," he said. "Misty Dawn's breathing on her own."

Miraculously, the rescue team had saved her.

Misty Dawn lives today because of the selfless work of Coast Guard rescue men and women. More than 7,000 lives are saved each year through Guard work. And Misty's call was only one of 71,000 that the Service answers each year. On the average, the Coast Guard saves a life every 75 minutes.

Search and rescue missions receive the most headlines of all Coast Guard work, and rescue crews have many dramatic stories to tell. The crews hone their skills through frequent practice. Rescue work is sometimes fatal, but the men and women take the risk even knowing this. Here too, the key word is teamwork, and helping people is the first priority. In addition to Alaska, the Coast Guard maintains search and

60

rescue units on the East, West, and Gulf coasts, as well as on Hawaii and the Great Lakes. The Service is tied into the AMVER System (Automated Mutual-assistance VEssel Rescue System) which uses satellites to pick up signal locations of vessels or aircraft in distress.

Most rescues use special helicopters, planes, or boats, but occasionally a rescue occurs using an unusual mode of transportation. In February 1986, a Coast Guardsman in California tied his surfboard to the rail of his rescue boat, paddled on the board through turbulent waters to the victims, and used the board to carry them to safety.

**Two boats from the Coast Guard Lifeboat School battle heavy waves and submerged rocks in a practice rescue situation. Such practice sessions can be nearly as dangerous as the real thing.**

## Protecting the Environment

Saving the environment is not a new idea. By order of Congress, the Cutter Service was protecting live oak trees over 150 years ago. Seals and whales, at one time close to extinction, owe their survival in part to the Service for its seagoing protection. The thriving sponge industry around Florida and the Gulf of Mexico has been protected since 1900. Throughout the twentieth century, people have become increasingly aware of the environment. Where possible, steps have been taken to save the environment for an ever-growing population.

When a ship explodes, burns, or wrecks in the water, it leaks its liquids into the environment. The pollution might be chemicals, acids, oil, gasoline, or some other type of dangerous cargo. These wastes then become a threat to marine life, birds, and people. To help clean up such a mess, the Coast Guard has created the highly trained unit called Strike Force. Much like a unit of the fire department, this force responds to alarms anywhere in the country. Its ranks include divers and marine salvage teams. The environmental Strike Force teams are so well-trained and efficient that other nations borrow them when confronted with a pollution problem—whether the emergency is on the water or not.

## Ice and the Weather

A year after an iceberg sank the *Titanic* in 1912, the Coast Guard took on another job. The United States, joined by other nations that used the North Atlantic sea lanes, formed the International Ice Patrol (the IIP).

Icebergs, mainly from the Greenland area, break off and begin a 2,000-3,000 mile journey along the Labrador Current into the shipping lanes of the North Atlantic. These bergs, some of which are a mile thick, are 80 percent hidden under water. They drift along as huge as buildings and as dangerous to ships as a hurricane. Some icebergs take up to a year to reach the Grand Banks of Newfoundland, Canada. When these masses drift through the blankets of fog, the scene for a disaster is complete.

Today, C-130 aircraft have replaced the 100-foot cutters used in earlier patrols. The new planes are able to range farther and faster than cutters and can oversee a larger area. In 1987, the IIP, in cooperation with the Canadian Ice Patrol, took a preseason (before March) count of icebergs around Greenland. They noted 3,400 in the area, 600 of which they predicted would eventually enter the southern shipping lanes.

The United States Coast Guard is developing a satellite tracking system that will give more accurate information on iceberg-carrying currents off Newfoundland. In this program, 500-pound, 12-foot-long buoys are launched from aircraft into the water. The buoys follow along the currents for up to a year, sending out information up to 10 times daily. This data is processed by a satellite, which beams the information to the program headquarters at Air Station Elizabeth City in New Jersey.

Drifting icebergs may not be a problem on the Great Lakes of North America, but winter ice certainly poses a threat there. Since these inland lakes connect the United States and Canada, a great deal of shipping traffic moves back and forth on them. It is important that these "roads" be kept open.

The Coast Guard icebreaker *Polar Star* passes a mammoth iceberg while sailing near Antarctica.

The Great Lakes are huge. They contain one-fourth of the world's fresh water! Superior is the largest, with Huron running a close second. Huron is about the size of West Virginia. It was Lake Huron that kept the Canadian and U.S. Coast Guards extra busy in March of 1987.

The winter had been mild, due to above-average temperatures and below-average snowfall. The breaking ice blocked the St. Clair River in March. That was normal—part of the icebreaking cycle every spring.

But a quick thaw followed by gale force winds loosened Huron ice sooner than usual. Great chunks of ice caused heavy flooding and massive river blockages. Icebreaking vessels worked from dawn until long into the night, backing and ramming, clearing, and keeping the water flowing. At one point, seven Coast Guard vessels were on duty, with *Mackinaw* serving as on-scene commander, and aircraft from Air Station Detroit spotting overhead. Sometimes *Mackinaw* fought its way through 15-foot-deep concentrations of ice. Although flooding was extensive during the month-long struggle, there's no telling what damage or death would have been caused had not the Coast Guard been on the scene.

The Great Lakes are not the only large icebreaking arena. The Coast Guard is responsible for icebreaking in the polar regions, too. Take, for instance, the 399-foot icebreaker *Polar Star*, home port Seattle, Washington. This red-hulled cutter was especially constructed for its ice duties. The shell plating and interior structure are made of special steel. The bow curves in such a way as to ride up onto the ice. With the power of the engines and the sturdy hull, the ship can ram its way through ice 21 feet thick—groaning and creaking all the while.

## Aids to Navigation

With the responsibility to maintain aids to navigation, the Coast Guard story comes full circle. Navigational aids include lighthouses, floating buoys, right-of-way markers—almost any "signpost" placed on water to inform ships of location or danger.

When the Lighthouse Service joined the Coast Guard in 1939, it brought with it the hardships and glories of the United States lighthouse keepers, who were around as early as 1716. Most lighthouses of the past were actually huge lanterns, lit and tended by hand. Today batteries and solar energy replace the old oil, fire, and wick. Besides batteries and solar power, electronic systems—such as satellites, radar, and LORAN—provide weather information and guide ships and aircraft much more efficiently.

The Coast Guard has a fleet of buoy-tending vessels (called the "black fleet" because of their black hulls) to keep the navigational aids in proper condition. These vessels range from 180-foot ocean-going ships down to the small 21-footers. Even the Mississippi River area, far from salt water, hosts buoy "tenders" stationed at such places as Buchanan, Tennessee; Omaha, Nebraska; St. Louis, Missouri; and Dubuque, Iowa.

Servicing navigational aids is an endless, ever-changing job. Nature continually alters coastlines, rivers, and channels. Electronics aboard the tender ships help to locate an aid and to see if it is in the right position. The Coast Guard is on the job to reposition such aids and to maintain them against the winds and sea.

All told, there are more than 48,000 aids to navigation along United States coastlines, lakes, and rivers. Some are lighted floating buoys, some are shore markers dotting the waterways. If these aids were located around the equator, there would be enough to place one every half mile.

The men and women who maintain the navigational aids for the U.S. will never see their names in the headlines. Like many Coast Guard activities, their mission *prevents* accidents and deaths.

Buoy tenders—or "tenders" in Coast Guard slang—are outfitted with many different kinds of equipment, so that their crew members are prepared for a number of tasks.

A small boat from the cutter *Firebush* hooks a tow line to a buoy. Coast Guard personnel perform their duties in some of the most beautiful parts of the world—not the least of the benefits the Service has to offer.

# Conclusion

A Coast Guard bumper sticker sums up the Service in a few words:

"Small Service. Big Job."

No other branch of the armed forces is asked to do so much with so little. The most important thing to remember about the Coast Guard is that its duties never stop—whether the U.S. is at war or at peace, the Coast Guard functions at full capacity. Within U.S. waters, any ship that sends an SOS, any smuggling or illegal operations at sea, any search-and-rescue operation, navigational marker, dangerous cargo, or chemical spill falls within the responsibilities of the Service.

If you are over 17, and you decide to find out more about the Coast Guard, your local recruiter is the person to see. He or she will give you the most up-to-date information about salaries, benefits, and opportunities for travel. Be sure to ask them *all* of the questions you can think of, because joining any branch of the service is an important decision. You need first to be well-informed; then you should discuss the idea with your parents, or possibly your guidance counselor at school. If you eventually decide that the Coast Guard is right for you, you'll be in very good company.

# Appendix

Coast Guard officers and enlisted personnel use approximately the same rank system as the U.S. Navy. List A shows the ranks for enlisted personnel (those who sign up with a recruiter) in order from lowest to highest. List B shows the ranks for officers (personnel who are commissioned, or given special training, either at the Coast Guard Academy or at Officer's Candidate School).

*List A*
Seaman Recruit
Seaman Apprentice
Seaman
Petty Officer Third Class
Petty Officer Second Class
Petty Officer First Class
Chief Petty Officer
Senior Chief Petty Officer
Master Chief Petty Officer
Master Chief Petty Officer of the Coast Guard
*List B*
Ensign
Lieutenant Junior Grade
Lieutenant
Lieutenant Commander
Commander
Captain
Rear Admiral (lower half)
Rear Admiral (upper half)
Vice Admiral
Admiral

# Index

*Photo Credits*

Photos courtesy of: U.S. Coast Guard, pp. 8, 11, 17, 19, 21, 23, 25, 27, 29 (both), 32, 33, 40, 44, 46, 48, 49 (all), 51, 61, 67, 68, *back cover*; Travel Information Division, Department of Conservation and Development, Raleigh, North Carolina, p. 22 (both); Paul Bobkowski, pp. 5, 54; Steamship Historical Society Collection, University of Baltimore Library, p. 14; J.L. Snyder, pp. 24, 43 (center), 53; Dennis Schaefer, p. 39; Ed Moreth, pp. 13, 58, 64; Christopher Haley, *cover*. Photos on pages 36, 37, and 43 (top and bottom) by Nancy Warren Ferrell.

*Front cover photo by Christopher Haley; back cover photo courtesy of U.S. Coast Guard.*